Nita Me...
Soups Salads & Starters

Nita Mehta

B.Sc. (Home Science), M.Sc. (Food and Nutrition), Gold Medalist

Co author
Harveen Choudhary

SNAB
Publishers Pvt Ltd

Nita Mehta's SOUPS, SALADS & STARTERS

© Copyright 1996-2002 **SNAB** Publishers Pvt Ltd

WORLD RIGHTS RESERVED. The contents—all recipes, photographs and drawings are original and copyrighted. No portion of this book shall be reproduced, stored in a retrieval system or transmitted by any means, electronic, mechanical, photocopying, recording or otherwise, without the written permission of the publishers.

While every precaution is taken in the preparation of this book, the publisher and the author assume no responsibility for errors or omissions. Neither is any liability assumed for damages resulting from the use of information contained herein.

TRADEMARKS ACKNOWLEDGED. Trademarks used, if any, are acknowledged as trademarks of their respective owners. These are used as reference only and no trademark infringement is intended upon.

6th Reprint 2002
ISBN 81-86004-15-7

Food Styling and Photography: **SNAB**

Layout and laser typesetting :

National Information Technology Academy
3A/3, Asaf Ali Road
☎ 3252948   New Delhi-110002

Published by :

SNAB
Publishers Pvt. Ltd.
3A/3 Asaf Ali Road,
New Delhi - 110002
Tel: 3252948, 3250091
Telefax:91-11-3250091

Editorial and Marketing office:
E-348, Greater Kailash-II, N.Delhi-48
*Fax:*91-11-6235218 *Tel:*91-11-6214011, 6238727
E-Mail: nitamehta@email.com
snab@snabindia.com
*Website:*http://www.nitamehta.com
Website: http://www.snabindia.com

Distributed by :
THE VARIETY BOOK DEPOT
A.V.G. Bhavan, M 3 Con Circus,
New Delhi - 110 001
Tel : 3327175, 3322567; Fax : 3714335

Printed by :
THOMSON PRESS (INDIA) LIMITED

Rs. 89/-

Foreword

There is nothing more pleasing than a hot soup to warm and cheer you up on a cold wintry day and nothing better than a chilled cold soup to cool you down on a hot summer day.

A salad can be an appetizer, a side dish, a snack or a main course. So say good bye to the traditional salads and say hello to the unusual. The recipes are created to give pleasure to the most discriminating tastes and add splendor, colour & excitement to every meal. However, keeping in with today's demand, the use of heavy creams & thickening agents have been kept to a minimum. In most of the soups, vegetables themselves have been used as thickening agents. The soups given here are all simple and quick to prepare.

Some unusual starters/accompaniments are included to go with your soups & salads.

Nita Mehta

English - Hindi Names

English	Hindi
Coriander	Dhania
Ginger	Adrak
Garlic	Lasan
Cottage Cheese	Paneer
Bay Leaf	Tej Patta
Cinnamon	Dalchini
Kidney Beans	Rajmah
Flour	Maida
Mint	Poodina
Dill	Soye
Cumin	Jeera
Nutmeg	Jaiphal
Lettuce Leaves	Salad Leaves
Soda-bicarb	Mitha Soda

Terms used in Cooking

Blanch	Put food in boiling water to remove skin
Blend	To mix all ingredients thoroughly until smooth & uniform
Colander	A vessel having holes at the bottom used as a strainer
Chill	To cool in the freezer compartment of the refrigerator without freezing
Garnish	Decorate
Mince	Cut with a very sharp knife into extremely small pieces
Puree	A smooth mixture obtained by blending in the mixer or passing through a sieve
Saute	To stir food quickly in hot oil or butter until soft but not brown
Simmer	Cook in water on very low fire below the boiling point
Strain	To pass through a sieve
Toss	To mix lightly

Contents

DIPS, PARTY STARTERS & UNUSUAL SOUPS

ACCOMPANIMENTS   112

Some Favourite
Soups

Cheese Soup

Picture on page 35

Serves 5-6

2 onions - chopped
2 tbsp oil or butter
3 medium potatoes - peeled & chopped
5 cups water
1 cup milk
½ cup sour cream

OR

½ cup fresh cream mixed with 1 tsp lemon juice
1 tsp salt & ½ tsp black pepper - to taste
1 cube (25 gm) cheese - grated

GARNISHING
1 toasted slice
1 cube (25 gm) cheese
fresh coriander leaves

1. In a pressure cooker add butter or oil and brown onions lightly.
2. Add potatoes & saute for 1-2 minutes. Add 5 cups water and give 3-4 whistles to the cooker. Remove from fire.
3. When cooled, blend the pressure cooked onion & potatoes in a mixer to a puree, along with all the water that was used for cooking them.
4. Strain the puree through a strainer. Keep aside.
5. Boil 1 cup milk separately in a clean pan.
6. Boil the soup separately. Keeping the soup on very low flame (the **soup should not be boiling**) add the boiled milk, **stirring continuously.** Simmer for 2-3 minutes on low flame.
7. Add grated cheese. Add salt & pepper to taste.
8. Add sour cream, keeping the flame **on very low heat & stirring continuously.** Remove the soup from fire.
9. To serve, grate cheese on a toasted slice of bread & put in an oven for a few minutes (or microwave it for a few seconds). Cut diagonally to form small triangles. Arrange a coriander leaf on each piece.
10. Heat the soup till it just starts to boil. Pour into bowls or cups and put 1-2 pieces of cheese triangles in each serving. Serve.

Lentil & Palak Soup

A light, nutritious soup with self garnishing.

Serves 6-7

2 medium/1 cup carrot - chopped
½ of a tiny bottle gourd (lauki, dudhi) - chopped (1 cup)
1 cup cabbage - chopped
1 medium capsicum - deseeded & chopped
2 tbsp moong dhuli dal
2 tbsp masoor dhuli dal
1½ tsp salt & ½ tsp pepper - to taste
5 cups water
juice of ½ lemon

GARNISHING
2½ cups spinach - stalk removed, leaves chopped fine, washed & drained
1 tbsp butter

1. Put all the vegetables and dals except spinach and lemon juice in a pressure cooker. Add 5 cups water and give 4-5 whistles. Remove from fire.
2. When the pressure comes down, blend the vegetables along with the water in a mixer to a puree.
3. Sieve the puree through a soup strainer.
4. Add juice of ½ lemon, salt & pepper to taste. Mix well. Keep the soup aside.
5. Heat butter in a frying pan, add drained chopped spinach and saute the spinach for 3-4 minutes.
6. Add the sauted spinach to the soup.
7. Boil soup and serve. There is no need for garnishing as it is already garnished with the spinach.

Tomato Shorba

Picture on page 17

A thin tomato soup with the authentic Indian flavour.

Serves 8

1 kg (12 medium) red tomatoes - chopped roughly
400 ml (2½ cups) water
2 tsp besan (gram flour)
1 cup dessicated coconut (nariyal ka burada) or freshly grated coconut
1 tbsp oil, 1 tsp jeera (cumin seeds)
8-10 curry leaves
2-3 green chillies - slit lengthways
1 tsp sugar - to taste, salt to taste
1 tsp lemon juice - to taste

GARNISHING

1 tbsp finely chopped fresh coriander leaves
2-3 tbsp boiled rice - optional

Cabbage & Coconut Salad : Page 85, Tomato Shorba : Page 16

1. Pressure cook the tomatoes with water to give one whistle. Keep on low flame for 5-7 minutes. Remove from fire.
2. After the pressure drops, strain the tomato juice. Mash well with a kadchi to extract all the juice. Keep aside.
3. Grate 1 cup of fresh coconut. Blend it with its own water in a mixer. If fresh coconut is not available, blend 1 cup dessicated coconut (nariyal ka burada) with 2 cups hot water in a mixer. Strain to extract milk. Put the unstrained coconut again in the blender with more hot water and churn again. Strain again. Repeat with more water if desired to get 4½ cups coconut milk in all.
4. Add besan to the coconut milk & blend well in the mixer. Keep aside.
5. Heat the oil in a pan & add the jeera. After it splutters, add curry leaves, green chillies, tomato juice, coconut milk & sugar.
6. Add salt to taste & cook for 4-5 minutes. Add lemon juice to taste. Garnish with coriander leaves and a few grains of boiled rice. Serve hot.

Mushroom Soup : Page 26, Moong Sprout Salad : Page 82

Mixed Vegetable Soup

A soup for the winter days when vegetables are in plenty!

Serves 6-8

VEGETABLE STOCK
3 onions - chopped
3 potatoes - chopped
3 tomatoes - chopped
7 cups water

OTHER INGREDIENTS
1 tbsp butter
2 tbsp finely chopped cabbage
2 tbsp fine flowerets of a cauliflower
¼ cup shelled peas
2 tbsp finely chopped carrots
2 tbsp finely chopped french beans
2 tbsp cornflour dissolved in 1 cup water
salt, pepper to taste

1. To prepare the vegetable stock, pressure cook all ingredients of the vegetable stock together for 10 minutes. Remove from fire.
2. Strain through a soup strainer. Keep the stock aside.
3. Heat butter. Add all the other vegetables and saute for 2 minutes.
4. Add the prepared stock. Boil.
5. Add the cornflour mixture, stirring continuously.
6. Add salt and pepper.
7. Cook for 5-7 minutes till the soup turns thick and creamy. Serve hot.

Cream of Almond

Picture on page 72

An economical, yet delicious, almond soup.

Serves 4

20 almonds (blanched) - chopped
1½ cups (½ small) cauliflower - remove stalk & break into tiny florets
1 tbsp oil / butter
3 cups water
1½ cups milk
1 tsp salt & ½ tsp pepper, or to taste

GARNISHING

some fresh dhania leaves (coriander) - chopped
a few blanched & finely chopped almonds

1. In a pressure cooker heat 1 tbsp oil and saute the tiny florets of cauliflower for 3-4 minutes on low flame.
2. Add 3 cups water and give 3-4 whistles. Remove from fire.
3. In a liquidiser or a small grinder, put **blanched** (**skin removed** by soaking in hot water), chopped almonds with ½ cup milk and blend them well to a smooth thin paste. Remove the almond milk from the grinder and add 1 more cup of milk. Keep aside.
4. When the cooker cools down, put the cauliflower along with all the water in the mixer and churn till it turns into a smooth puree.
5. Mix cauliflower puree and almond milk together. Boil.
6. Add salt & pepper to taste. Garnish with coriander leaves and a few almonds if desired. Serve hot.

Tomato Rasam

A simple South Indian soup with a distinctive flavour.

Serves 4

4 large tomatoes - whole
3 cups water
¼ tsp haldi (turmeric powder)
¼ tsp hing (asafoetida powder)
1½ tsp salt, or to taste
coriander leaves for garnishing
a tiny piece gur (jaggery)

RASAM POWDER
5 whole, dry red chillies
3 tsp coriander seeds
½ tsp jeera (cumin seeds)
¼ tsp sarson (mustard powder)
few curry leaves
1 tsp oil

1. Boil the tomatoes on low flame with 1 cup of water for 10 minutes, till they turn soft. Remove from fire & cool.
2. Add 2 cups of water. Mash lightly. **Do not put in a blender.** Strain the tomato puree. Keep aside.
3. Fry all the ingredients of the rasam powder on very low flame, for 3-4 minutes till the smell of the masalas comes. Remove from fire and powder it finely.
4. To the tomato puree, add salt, gur and haldi powder. Boil.
5. Add rasam powder and hing. Cook for 1-2 minutes. Remove from fire.
6. Garnish with coriander leaves.

Mushroom Soup

Picture on page 18

A splendid soup for the mushroom lovers.

Serves 5

75 gms mushrooms (8-9 pieces) - chopped finely
1 big onion - chopped finely
5 level tbsp maida (plain flour)
2 cups milk
6 cups water
4 tbsp butter
1½ tsp salt
½ tsp pepper - to taste
½" piece ginger - chopped
1 tbsp cornflour dissolved in ¼ cup water

GARNISHING
green leaves of spring onions - cut into very fine round slices

1. Heat ½ tbsp butter. Add onions and ginger. Cook for 2 minutes on low flame, until onions turn transparent.
2. Add milk and water. Boil. Keep on low flame for 2 minutes. Strain. Keep aside.
3. Saute mushrooms in 3½ tbsp butter for 2-3 minutes on low flame.
4. Reduce flame. Add maida & stir fry for 1 minute on low flame.
5. Add milk-water mixture. Boil. Add cornflour paste.
6. Add salt and pepper and cook for some time until the soup turns thick and creamy.
7. Serve hot, each cup garnished with 2-3 rings of spring onion tops or a coriander leaf.

Capsicum Flavoured Vegetable Soup

A thick, wholesome soup.

Serves 4

VEGETABLE STOCK
1 small onion - chopped
1 carrot - chopped
1/8 of a small cabbage - chopped
3 cups water

OTHER INGREDIENTS
1 tbsp butter
½ capsicum - deseeded & finely chopped
3-4 flakes garlic - minced finely
5-6 pepper corns (saboot kali mirch)
2-3 cloves (laung)
1 slice bread
salt & pepper to taste

1. To prepare the vegetable stock, pressure cook all ingredients of the vegetable stock together to give 3-4 whistles. Remove from fire. Keep aside.
2. To prepare the soup, heat butter. Reduce flame. Add garlic. Saute for ½ minute.
3. Add capsicum, pepper corns and cloves. Saute for ½ minute.
4. Cut bread into 8-10 pieces and add. Stir continuously on low flame for 1 minute. Remove from fire.
5. Transfer all the ingredients of the stock in the cooker to a blender. Add the capsicum-bread mixture also to the blender. Blend both together to get a thick, smooth soup. Remove the soup in a pan.
6. Give it one boil. Add salt and pepper to taste. If it appears extra thick, add more water and give it 2-3 boils to get the desired consistency.

Spinach Soup

Picture on page 71

Serves 4-5

3 cups chopped spinach (palak)
3 cups water
¼ " piece ginger - chopped, 1-2 flakes garlic, 1 tej patta (bay leaf)
1 cup milk, salt & pepper to taste

GARNISHING
½ cup crumbled cottage cheese (roughly mashed paneer)
1 tsp lemon juice

1. Boil chopped spinach with bay leaf, garlic, ginger & 3 cups water. Cover & simmer for 7-8 minutess. Puree in a blender & **sieve**. Add salt & pepper to taste. Boil the spinach puree for 2-3 minutes.
2. Add milk, stirring continuously. Boil again. Remove from fire. Add lemon juice, stirring continuously.
3. To serve, boil soup. Garnish with crumbled paneer & serve.

Vegetable Broth

A thick, low calorie, nutritive soup.

Serves 4

1½ cups (½ of a small cauliflower) cauliflower chopped (without stalk)
1 turnip (shalgam) - chopped, ¼ of a small cabbage - chopped
4 cups water, 1 cup milk
salt & pepper to taste
1 tsp kasoori methi (dried fenugreek leaves) - stems removed
a few pepper corns (saboot kali mirch) - coarsely powdered to garnish

1. Pressure cook cauliflower, cabbage & turnip together with 4 cups water to give 3-4 whistles.
2. When the pressure drops, mash the vegetables well with a potato masher to a puree. The soup is not to be very smooth, that is why the vegetables are not mixed in a blender.
3. Add milk, kasoori methi, salt & pepper. Boil for 2-3 minutes. Serve hot, sprinkling each serving with a pinch of coarsely powdered pepper corns.

French Onion Soup

Serves 4

3 tbsp butter
2 onions - sliced very finely
4 flakes garlic - crushed
1½ tbsp flour (maida)
salt and black pepper powder to taste
4 cups stock (given below) or water

STOCK

1 carrot - chopped roughly
1 onion - chopped roughly
2 bay leaves (tej patta)
6-7 pepper corns (saboot kali mirch)
4 cups water

GARNISHING

25 gm cheese - grated
½ tsp mustard powder, 1 slice of bread - toasted

1. To prepare the stock, pressure cook all ingredients of the stock with 4 cups water to give 3-4 whistles. Pass through a sieve. Keep stock aside.
2. Heat the butter in a clean, **heavy bottomed** pan. Fry the onions and garlic over a moderately low heat, stirring occasionally to prevent sticking, until **brown. Do not let the onions burn.**
3. Add the flour and cook for 1 minute on low flame. Pour in the stock gradually, stirring continuously. Boil. Season with salt and pepper, and simmer for 5 minutes. Keep soup aside.
4. To garnish the soup, mix the mustard powder and cheese together in a small bowl. Blend well. Spread over the toasted bread. Place the toasted slice in the oven for a few minutes. Cut into 4 squares.
5. Serve steaming hot soup with one piece of cheese toast in each serving.

Creamy Onion Soup

Serves 4

2 onions - thinly sliced or finely chopped
2 tbsp oil
1 tbsp flour (maida)
1 cup milk
4 cups water
1 bay leaf (tej patta)
1" stick of cinnamon (dalchini)
½ tsp mustard powder
1 tsp salt - to taste
½ tsp pepper - to taste

GARNISHING
25 gm (1 cube) cheese - grated
fresh coriander leaves

Beet root & Baby Onion Salad : Page 102, Cheese Soup : Page 12

1. In a pressure cooker heat oil and fry onions till golden brown.
2. Add bay leaf & cinnamon stick.
3. Add flour and fry for 1-2 minutes, stirring continuously.
4. Add water and give 2-3 whistles. Remove from fire.
5. When cool, open the cooker and add mustard powder, salt & pepper to taste.
6. Add milk. Discard the bay leaf and cinnamon stick. Boil.
7. Serve very hot garnished with grated cheese and fresh coriander leaves.

Crunchy Rolls : Page 115, Cheese Dip : Page 113

Cream of Tomato Soup

The perfect tomato soup!

Serves 8

1 kg (12 medium) red tomatoes
1 carrot - chopped, 1 onion - chopped, 1 potato - chopped
4-5 laung (cloves)
4-5 saboot kali mirch (pepper corns)
1" stick of dalchini (cinnamon)
2 tbsp butter
2 tsp salt, 1-2 tsp sugar
2 tbsp cornflour

GARNISHING

4-5 tbsp cream
bread croutons (deep fried tiny bread cubes)

OR

tiny cubes of paneer
fresh coriander leaves - chopped

1. Heat butter in a pressure cooker. Add onion, carrot, potato, laung, saboot kali mirch and dalchini. Cook until onion turns pale and transparent.
2. Add washed whole tomatoes.
3. Add 6 cups water and pressure cook to give two whistles. Remove from fire.
4. Mash the tomatoes slightly and strain.
5. Churn the unstrained part in a mixer.
6. Strain again. Throw away the solid unstrained part.
7. Keep the soup on fire. Boil, stirring occasionally.
8. Add 2 tbsp cornflour dissolved in half a cup of water.
9. Add salt, pepper and sugar and cook for 5-7 minutes.
10. Serve hot garnished with few croutons & a swirl of cream, or coriander leaves and paneer pieces.

Note: To make croutons, cut 1 day old bread into small cubes and deep fry in hot oil.

Green Pea Soup

Serves 4

1 cup shelled peas
1 tbsp butter
1 onion - chopped, 3 flakes garlic - crushed
4 cups water, ½ cup milk
salt & pepper to taste, a pinch sugar
25 gm cheese - grated

1. Heat butter in a pressure cooker. Add garlic and onions. Cook till onions turn transparent.
2. Add peas. Saute for 2-3 minutes on low flame.
3. Add water. Give 3-4 whistles. Remove from fire. After it cools down, blend in a mixer to get a smooth puree. Strain the soup.
4. Add milk. Heat the soup & add salt & pepper to taste. Boil for 2 minutes.
5. To serve, boil soup. Keeping the flame low, add the grated cheese. Mix and serve hot.

Soups from
Far & Wide

Mexican Chilli Bean Soup

Serves 5-6

1 cup red kidney beans (rajmah)
1 tbsp oil
2-3 flakes garlic - crushed
4 cups water
2-3 spring onions - chopped
1 capsicum - deseeded & chopped
5 large tomatoes - pureed in a mixer
1 tsp red chilli powder
salt to taste
1-2 tbsp chilli sauce - to taste
1½ tsp dried oregano

OR
½ tsp powdered ajwain

GARNISHING
some grated cheese

1. Soak the beans overnight in water. Next day boil them with some water in a pressure cooker. Beans should turn very soft. Strain & mash beans coarsely with a spoon or a kadchi. Keep mashed beans aside.
2. Blend 5 tomatoes in a mixer to obtain puree. Strain the puree through a soup strainer & keep aside.
3. In a pan heat oil & fry garlic for 1-2 minutes on low flame.
4. Add spring onion & capsicum & fry for 2 minutes.
5. Add beans & all the other ingredients. Fry for another 1-2 minutes.
6. Add the strained tomato puree of 5 large tomatoes.
7. Add 4 cups of water and let it simmer for 5-7 minutes.
8. Serve hot garnished with grated cheese.

Vegetable Corn Soup

Picture on cover

Serves 8

1 tin corn (cream style) (3 cups)
2 tsp salt, or to taste, ¾ tsp white pepper
½ tsp ajinomoto
8 cups of water
½ carrot
¼ cup finely chopped greens of spring onions or capsicum
2 tbsp white vinegar, or to taste
4 level tbsp cornflour dissolved in 1 cup water
1 tsp soya sauce

1. Peel carrot and cut into thin long slices. Cut each slice into tiny cubes to get ½ cup of very finely chopped carrots. Cut only the greens of spring onions finely. Keep aside.
2. Put the tinned corn in a grinder and churn for a few seconds only to crush the corn slightly.
3. Remove corn from mixer and put in a heavy bottomed pan. Add 8 cups water. Add salt and pepper. Keep on fire and bring it to a boil.
4. Add ajinomoto. Mix.
5. Mix cornflour in 1 cup water and add to the corn mixture. Keep on boiling on low heat for 8-10 minutes till thick and creamy.
6. Add vinegar and carrots. Boil for 1 minute.
7. Add spring onion greens and soya sauce. Immediately remove from fire and serve with green chillies in vinegar.

Note: If you make half the quantity of soup, the left over tinned corn should be transferred to a steel or a plastic container and kept in the freezer. It stays for 20-30 days without getting spoilt.

Tom Yaam Pla

(Thai Hot & Sour Soup with Vegetables)

Serves 3-4

STOCK
3 cups chopped cabbage
2 tbsp chopped celery
1 stalk lemon grass
5 cups water

TO BE ADDED TO SOUP
3 tbsp bamboo shoot - cut into ½" pieces - optional
1 tbsp thin strips of ginger, (juliennes)
1 medium / 3 tbsp carrot - cut into 1" thin pieces, (juliennes)
5 large / 100 gms fresh mushrooms - cut into flat slices
2 tbsp basil (tulsi) leaves - optional
8-10 lemon leaves - optional
1 tbsp lemon juice
½ cup roasted peanuts - finely ground to a powder
1 tbsp oil, salt to taste

GRIND TO A PASTE
3 flakes garlic
2 tbsp chopped coriander leaves
4-5 pepper corns

GARNISHING
coriander or basil leaves

1. Put all the ingredients given under stock in a pressure cooker.
2. Give 3-4 whistles. When the pressure drops, strain the soup without mashing the vegetables, so as to get a clear soup. Keep aside.
3. In a pan put oil & fry the garlic, coriander & pepper corn paste for 1-2 minutes. Add all the other vegetables and again fry for 1-2 minutes.
4. Add basil & lemon leaves if available.
5. Add the stock that was prepared in steps 1 & 2.
6. Add lemon juice, salt & peanut powder.
7. Let the soup simmer for 15-20 minutes.
8. Serve hot garnished with coriander.

Note: If you like a thicker soup, add 1 tbsp cornflour mixed with ¼ cup water. Boil for 2-3 minutes on low flame after adding cornflour.

Man Chow Soup

Serves 5-6

3 flakes of garlic - chopped fine
½" ginger piece - chopped fine
1½ tbsp oil
1 tbsp soya sauce
¼ tsp ajinomoto
½ - 1 tsp salt - (to taste)
½ tsp white pepper
1 tbsp chilli sauce
½ tomato - very finely chopped
½ cabbage - very finely chopped
1 cup mushrooms or chicken cut into small pieces
6 cups vegetable stock (given below) or water
5-6 tbsp cornflour dissolved in ½ cup water

GARNISHING
noodles - deep fried

VEGETABLE STOCK (OPTIONAL)
1 onion - chopped, 1 carrot - chopped
4-5 french beans - threaded & chopped
½ tsp ginger - crushed, ½ tsp garlic - crushed
1 small potato - peeled & chopped
6 cups of water

1. You may use 6 cups of **water instead of the vegetable stock.** To prepare the vegetable stock, pressure cook all chopped vegetables of the stock and water together to give a whistle. After the first whistle keep on low flame for 15-20 minutes. Remove from fire. Cool. Strain to get a clear stock.
2. Heat oil. Add chopped ginger & garlic & fry on low flame for 1 minute.
3. Add tomatoes and fry till tomatoes turn soft and get cooked.
4. Add all the other vegetables and fry for 1-2 minutes.
5. Add all seasonings and the stock. Simmer after the first boil. Add cornflour dissolved in water & simmer on low flame for 8-10 minutes.
6. Sprinkle coriander leaves and serve topped some with fried noodles.

Australian Garlic Bread Soup

A delicious soup prepared out of your everyday bread.

Serves 4-5

4 flakes garlic - chopped
4 slices of bread
2 tbsp butter
2 medium size tomatoes
2 cups milk
salt & pepper to taste
4 cups water

GARNISHING
1 tomato - deseeded & chopped very fine

1. Break the bread into small pieces.
2. Peel and chop the tomatoes into small pieces.
3. In a pressure cooker heat the butter and saute garlic for 1-2 minutes, on low flame.
4. Add bread pieces and fry them for 1-2 minutes on low flame, stirring continuously.
5. Add chopped tomatoes, salt, pepper and 4 cups of water.
6. Give 2-3 whistles. Remove from fire.
7. When cool, pour into a mixer and blend well.
8. Add 1 cup of milk. Strain to remove the seeds of tomatoes. Keep aside.
9. To serve, heat the soup well but do not let it boil. Stir continuously while heating the soup.
10. Garnish with very finely chopped & deseeded tomato pieces.

Note: This soup becomes very thick on keeping. If this happens add more milk just before serving.

Chinese Hot & Sour Soup

For a good soup, all vegetables in the soup should be very finely shredded.

Serves 5-6

VEGETABLE STOCK
1 good size onion - chopped
1 carrot - chopped
4-5 french beans
½ tsp ginger - crushed
½ tsp garlic - crushed
1 small potato - peeled & chopped
5-6 cups of water

VEGETABLES
4 tbsp finely shredded mushrooms
5 tbsp finely shredded cabbage
5 tbsp finely shredded carrots

Russian Salad : Page 108

2 tbsp finely shredded french beans
2 tbsp finely shredded capsicum
100 gms paneer - cubed in small pieces
4 tbsp cornflour dissolved in ½ cup water
1 egg (optional)
½ tsp sugar, ½ tsp ajinomoto, ½ tsp chilli sauce
1 tsp black pepper & salt
3 tbsp vinegar, 3 tsp soya sauce (add more for a darker colour)
1 tbsp chopped celery -optional
2 tbsp oil
2 tbsp tomato puree

GARNISHING

In a spoon heat 1 tsp oil. Add ½ tsp red chilli powder & pour on top of the soup.

Macaroni & Peanut Salad : Page 84, Italian Dressing : Page 77

1. To prepare the vegetable stock, pressure cook chopped vegetables and water together to give one whistle.
2. After the first whistle keep on low flame for 10 minutes. Remove from fire. Cool. Strain to get a clear stock. **Do not mash the vegetables**. Discard vegetables & keep stock aside.
3. In a pan heat oil. Add 2 tbsp tomato puree. Fry for 1 minute.
4. Add all the shredded vegetables & mushrooms. Fry for 3-4 minutes.
5. Add soya sauce & fry for 2-3 minutes on low flame. (This gives the dark colour to the soup).
6. Add salt, pepper, sugar, ajinomoto, vinegar, paneer pieces & stock.
7. After one boil let it simmer on low heat for 5-6 minutes.
8. Mix cornflour in ½ cup water and add to soup. Bring to a boil.
9. If using egg, beat the egg well with a fork. Pour into boiling soup through a fine sieve, stirring constantly.
10. At serving time, boil the soup well. To garnish, heat 1 tsp oil in a kadchi or a big spoon. Remove spoon from fire. Add ½ tsp red chilli powder & pour the chilli oil on top of the soup.
11. Serve with green chillies in vinegar, chilli sauce & soya sauce.

Cold Soups

Strawberry Delight

A delightful soup which can also be served as a punch/drink.

Serves 4-5

10-12 strawberries pureed in the mixer

OR

1 cup strawberry puree
1 cup fresh cream
6 tbsp sugar
3 cups water
¾ tsp salt
1 tsp pepper
juice of ½ a lemon

GARNISHING
A few mint leaves

1. Wash and chop the strawberries.
2. Blend them in a mixer to a smooth puree. Keep the strawberry puree aside.
3. Heat sugar and water till sugar dissolves and the mixture boils. Cool the sugar syrup.
4. Mix sugar syrup, strawberry puree, salt, pepper & lemon juice in a mixer and blend for 3-4 minutes.
5. Add fresh cream and again blend for 1-2 minutes. More sugar may be added according to taste.
6. Serve chilled decorated with a mint leaf.

Cream of Walnuts

A great hit with walnut lovers.

Serves 4-5

2 cups low fat yoghurt (curd made from skimmed milk)
2 medium/2 cups cucumber - chopped
½ cup walnuts, 2 tsp fresh dill (soye leaves)- chopped
1-2 flakes garlic - crushed (optional)
salt to taste

1. Peel, deseed and chop the cucumbers into small pieces.
2. Coarsely powder the walnuts.
3. In a liquidizer add all the ingredients - curds, walnuts, cucumber, dill & garlic. Churn till nearly smooth.
4. Add salt to taste. Serve chilled.

Note:
- This soup does not require any garnishing as the dill present in it acts as a natural garnish.
- Instead of walnuts almonds can be used.

Chilled Cucumber-Yoghurt Soup

Even the kids love the coolness this soup imparts!

Serves 3-4

2 medium/2 cups chopped cucumber
½ cup water
½ cup low fat yoghurt (curds made from skimmed milk)
½ tbsp honey (adjust to taste)
1 flake garlic (optional)
salt to taste
5-6 fresh mint leaves (pudina)

GARNISHING
some mint leaves

1. Peel, deseed & chop cucumbers into small pieces.
2. In a liquidiser add yoghurt, cucumbers, water, honey, mint leaves, salt and garlic. Churn/blend till pureed well & smooth.
3. Strain the puree. Serve chilled, decorated with a mint leaf.

Cream of Summer Greens

Serves 2-3

1½ cups fresh spinach - chopped
½ cup chopped bottle gourd (louki, ghiya)
1 cup curd
1 cup lettuce (salad leaves) - chopped
salt & black pepper to taste

GARNISHING
some fresh coriander leaves - chopped
some green onions - finely chopped (optional)

1. Pressure cook ghiya and spinach with ½ cup water to give 3 whistles.
2. When cool, puree vegetables in a mixer along with the cooking water.
3. Puree the chopped lettuce with 1 cup curd separately. Blend till smooth.
4. Mix the pureed lettuce & vegetable puree together. Add salt & pepper. Serve chilled, garnished with coriander leaves & green onions.

Note: For a thinner soup increase curds or water & for a thicker one reduce water.

Cascadilla Chilled (Cream Tomato Soup)

Serves 4-5

4-5 medium tomatoes - chopped

OR

3 cups tomato juice
½ cup curd
½ capsicum - chopped, ½ cucumber - deseeded and chopped
1 green onion/spring onion - chopped
1 flake garlic - crushed (optional)
1 tbsp honey (adjust to your taste)
salt & pepper to taste

GARNISHING
a few mint leaves

1. If using fresh tomatoes, blend well in the mixer. Strain to get a clear juice.
2. Mix all the ingredients to the juice and blend well in the mixer till smooth.
3. Strain and serve very cold garnished with mint leaves.

Gazpacho

Serves 4-5

5 cups ready made tomato juice or 6-7 red tomatoes put whole in hot water for
10 minutes, pureed in a blender & strained to get juice
1 small onion - well minced
1 cup deseeded & finely chopped capsicum
2 tbsp vinegar
juice of ½ lemon
1 tbsp honey (adjust to your taste)
salt & pepper to taste
dash of ground cumin powder (jeera powder)
dash of tabasco sauce

GARNISHING
fresh coriander leaves - chopped

1. Combine all ingredients. Blend well in the mixer to a puree.
2. Strain the puree. Serve chilled, garnished with chopped fresh coriander.

Salads

Salad Dressings & Garnishes

To keep all vegetables crisp & fresh for the salad, they should be cut
& put in ice cold water for 10 minutes. These should then be strained
through a large strainer (colander) & put on a clean kitchen towel to
absorb all the excess water. Never squeeze the vegetables.
When mixing a dressing with a salad, always keep the raw vegetables
& fruits in a large bowl. Pour a little dressing and toss (mix) lightly
with 2 forks, holding one in each hand. Add the dressing gradually to
see how much more dressing is required. Too much dressing added to
a salad does not taste as well as look good. The dressing should be
just enough to coat the vegetables lightly.

Fancy Salad Garnishes

Lemon Twists

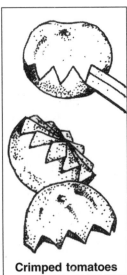

Crimped tomatoes

Radish Roses & Accordians

Fancy Salad Garnishes

Put these garnishes in ice cold water & keep them dipped in chilled water in the fridge for several hours or even overnight.

Tomato Rose: Peel a firm, red tomato with a sharp knife, round and round (all around the tomato) to get a ¾" broad strip. If the peel breaks in-between, never mind. Just continue till the end. Remember to keep the width of the peel **uneven** while peeling, to make it look like petals. Roll the strips to make a rose. Arrange 2-3 mint or coriander leaves (dipped in ice cold water for 15 min), on the sides.

Lemon Rose: If you want to add a dash of yellow to a salad, make a rose with the lemon peel from a firm, big, yellow lemon, in the same way as above.

Lemon, Orange or Musambi Twists: Cut a slightly thick unpeeled slice. Make a cut from any point, only till the centre. Twist the slice a little & chill in iced water. Fruits with a thicker peel make better twists.

Borders: Unpeeled orange, musambi, cucumber or lemon slices can be made into beautiful edgings. If these fruits have a green peel, it adds to the beauty of the border.

Parsley: If available, the curly leaves placed at intervals in small bunches, enhances the beauty of the salads.

Carrot sticks: Cut carrot into long thin strips and chill in ice water.

Carrot curls: Peel long paper thin slices with a potato peeler. Roll each strip around the finger, fasten with toothpicks and chill in iced water.

Radish roses: Partially peel outside rosy skin to form rose petals.

Radish accordians: Give **close shallow** cuts & chill in ice water.

Spring onion flowers: Cut the green part of the onion, leaving 1½" of the green stem. Peel the bulb (white part) nicely. Cut the bulb into many sections, only till the white part, leaving the green part intact. Chill in iced water.

Salad

Dressings

Vegetarian Mayonnaise (eggless)

Gives 1½ cups dressing

1 cup milk
1 tbsp cornflour - dissolved in ½ cup cold milk
1 tbsp salad oil or any cooking oil
½ tsp sugar
1 tsp mustard powder
1 tbsp vinegar
1 tsp lemon juice
salt & pepper to taste
75 gms (½ cup) fresh cream

Sesame Potato Triangles : Page 119, Spinach Soup : Page 30

1. Boil 1 cup of milk in pan. Slow down the fire & add the cornflour mix, stirring continuously. Stir for 1-2 minutes till a smooth paste is ready.
2. Remove from fire & let it cool.
3. When cool, beat well with a whisk and add 1 tbsp oil gradually.
4. Add salt, pepper, sugar, mustard powder, lemon juice & vinegar. Mix well and chill in the fridge for 1-2 hours before using.
5. Lightly mix fresh cream after chilling the dressing.

VARIATIONS

- **Garlic Mayonnaise** - Crush 2-3 flakes of garlic and add to the prepared mayonnaise.
- **Minty Mayonnaise** - Add 6-8 crushed mint leaves to the prepared mayonnaise.
- **Green Mayonnaise** - Parboil & drain ½ cup spinach leaves. Puree in a mixer and add to the prepared mayonnaise.

Cream of Almond : Page 22, Spinach & Mushroom Salad : Page 80

Mayonnaise Sauce (with egg)

Gives 3/4 cup dressing

1 egg
½ cup any cooking oil
½ tsp mustard powder
1 tsp sugar
¼ tsp salt
¼ tsp pepper
1 tbsp vinegar

1. Add egg, sugar & mustard powder to the blender of your mixer. Churn for 1-2 minutes.
2. Keeping the blender on, add oil slowly spoonful by spoonful, churning all the time.
3. Keep adding oil gradually, till it starts to thicken. Once the sauce thickens slightly, keeping the blender on, pour the oil in a thin stream from the cup directly in larger quantities.
4. Churn till all the oil is used up & you get a thick mayonnaise dressing.

5. Add salt & vinegar. Churn once more.
6. Remove from mixer to a bowl. Chill for 1-2 hours before use.

Note: If the mayonnaise does not thicken or it curdles, remove from the blender into a cup. Break another egg into the empty blender. Churn. Keeping the blender on, add the old mayonnaise (in the cup), spoon by spoon, into the blender. Keep adding the old mayonnaise till all is used up & a new perfect mayonnaise is ready.

VARIATIONS

- **Garlic Mayonnaise** - Crush 3-4 flakes of garlic and add to the prepared mayonnaise.
- **Minty Mayonnaise** - Add 6-8 crushed mint leaves to the prepared mayonnaise.
- **Green Mayonnaise** - Parboil & drain 1 cup spinach leaves. Puree in a mixer and add to prepared mayonnaise.

French Dressing

Gives ½ cup dressing

4 tbsp salad oil or any cooking oil
4 tbsp white vinegar
½ tsp salt & pepper each
2 tsp sugar
3/4 tsp mustard
4 flakes of garlic crushed (optional)

1. Put all the ingredients in a mixer and blend patiently for **2-3 minutes or even more, till the dressing becomes slightly thick & creamy.**
2. Chill for 2-3 hours before using. Mix with raw vegetables - a combination of chopped kheera, tomato & roughly torn 1 cm pieces of cabbage.

Note: The dressing can be kept in an airtight container in the fridge for 5-6 days. Shake well before use. This dressing may be added to any fruit & vegetable mix to make it special.

Italian Dressing

Picture on page 54

Gives ½ cup dressing

1 tbsp less than ½ cup salad oil or any other refined cooking oil
1 tbsp lime juice, 2 tbsp white vinegar
2-3 flakes (¼ tsp) crushed garlic (optional)
2 tbsp chopped onion
½ tsp of each salt, sugar and mustard powder
½-1 tsp red chilli powder
1 tbsp of dried oregano (or ½ tsp ground ajwain can be used)
1 bay leaf (tej patta) - broken into pieces

1. Place all the ingredients in the mixer and blend patiently for **3-4 minutes till thick and creamy.** Chill for 2-4 hours before use.

Note: The dressing can be kept in an airtight container in the fridge for a week. Shake well before use. This dressing may be added to any fruit and vegetable mix to make it special.

Green Cottage Cheese Dressing

A unique, low calorie dressing.

Gives 1 cup

½ cup fresh cottage cheese (home made paneer made from ½ litre low fat milk
- reserve the whey, the greenish liquid)
½ green chilli - deseeded
¼ cup milk
1 tbsp vinegar, ½ tsp sugar
3 tbsp chopped coriander leaves
salt to taste

1. Make paneer from milk. Do not strain the paneer. Churn the paneer
   along with the water with all the other ingredients in the mixer for 2-3 min
   till smooth. Chill for 2-3 hours before use.

Note: This dressing is very thin when made but becomes thick upon chilling.
It should be used within 1-2 days of making.

Fancy/Party
Salads

Spinach & Mushroom Salad

Picture on page 72

Serves 3-4

30 leaves of spinach (stem removed) - shredded into thin strips
4 large salad or cabbage leaves - torn into 1" pieces with the hands
6 large fresh mushrooms

DRESSING

2 tbsp lemon juice (depending on taste)
2 flakes garlic - chopped / crushed (optional)
1 tsp mustard powder
2 tbsp oil
salt & pepper to taste

GARNISH

1 large tomato - cut into wedges

1. Wash the salad leaves and tear roughly into 1" pieces. Put in chilled water for 15 minutes.
2. Wash spinach leaves. Discard the stems and shred the leaves very finely. Put in chilled water for 15 minutes.
3. Wash mushrooms very well. Boil 2-3 cups water with ½ tsp sugar and ¼ tsp salt. Add washed mushrooms to the boiling water. Remove from fire after ½ minute. Strain. Put the mushrooms in cold water for 5 minutes to get refreshed. Strain. Cut the mushrooms with a sharp knife into very thin **'T'** shaped slices.
4. In a small bowl mix together all the ingredients of the dressing.
5. Keep the mushrooms, salad or cabbage leaves and spinach leaves in a bowl.
6. An hour before serving, add the dressing. Toss lightly. Chill for 1 hour before serving.
7. Decorate with tomato wedges.

Moong Sprout Salad

Picture on page 18

Serves 4-5

3 cups long sprouts of moong
½ small kheera (cucumber) - grated
1 capsicum - shredded into thin long strips
1 firm tomato - pulp removed & cut into thin long strips
18-20 black or green grapes - halved
juice of 1 lemon
2 tsp oil
salt to taste
½ tsp pepper
2 tsp honey
2" piece of ginger - grated & squeezed through a muslin cloth to get ginger juice

1. Boil 3-4 cups water in a pan. Put sprouts in a colander (abig flat steel strainer, normally used to strain boiled rice). Place the colander over the pan of boiling water & cover it. Steam for only 1-2 minutes till the sprouts turn slightly soft, but remain crunchy. Remove from fire. Keep the sprouts in the strainer for 5 minutes & then transfer on to a clean kitchen towel to absorb excess water.
2. Grate kheera. Sprinkle lemon juice over it.
3. In a large bowl, put sprouts. Sprinkle salt, honey & ginger juice over them and mix lightly.
4. Add grapes, capsicum, tomato strips and kheera along with the lemon juice.
5. Add salt, pepper and oil. Mix lightly with 2 forks. Serve chilled.

Macaroni & Peanut Salad

Picture on page 54

Serves 4-5

(100 gm) 1½ cups small macaroni
3-4 tbsp peanuts with red skin, ½ tsp oil
1 capsicum - cut into ¼" squares
1 recipe Italian dressing (½ cup) page - 77
1 unpeeled kheera (cucumber) - cut into neat round slices for garnishing

1. Prepare the dressing as given on page 77. Chill the dressing.
2. Boil 6-7 cups water with 2 tsp salt and 1 tbsp oil. Add macaroni and cook for 8-10 minutes, stirring occasionally till soft. Remove from fire and leave macaroni in hot water for about 2-3 minutes, till it swells properly. Strain. Put in cold water and strain again.
3. Saute peanuts in ½ tsp oil, stirring continuously, on low flame for a few minutes.
4. Mix capsicum, macaroni & peanuts together in a large bowl.
5. Pour the dressing and mix lightly. To garnish, make a border of unpeeled kheera slices.

Cabbage & Coconut Salad

Picture on page 17

Serves 4

½ of a firm, medium sized cabbage - shredded finely (hard core removed) &
dipped in ice cold water for 15 minutes
¼ of a fresh coconut - grated into long shreds
1 green chilli - deseeded, ¼ " piece ginger - chopped
¾ cup curd made from full cream milk - hung for ½ hour in a muslin cloth
2 tsp oil, ½ tsp mustard seeds (sarson), a few curry leaves

1. Remove shredded cabbage from cold water & put on a kitchen towel.
2. Grind half of the grated coconut, 1 green chilli & ¼ " ginger to a paste.
3. Mix cabbage, left over grated coconut & paste together in a large pan.
4. Beat hung curd till smooth & sprinkle curd on the cabbage with a tbsp, just enough to coat the cabbage lightly. Keep aside.
5. Heat oil in a small vessel. Reduce flame. Add mustard seeds. After they splutter, add curry leaves. Remove from fire & pour over cabbage. Mix well. Chill salad. At serving time, add ½ tsp salt & mix.

Vegetables in Light Mustard Dressing

Picture on cover

Serves 4

LIGHT MUSTARD DRESSING
½ cup thick curd - beat till smooth
2 flakes garlic - chopped finely
½ tbsp oil
¼ tsp crushed fresh peppercorns (saboot kali mirch)
½ tsp salt, ½ tsp sugar
2 tsp mustard paste, approx.

OTHER INGREDIENTS
2 slices tinned pineapple - cut into 1" pieces
4-5 olives or cherries, optional
3/4 cup carrots - cut into paper thin round slices (1 large carrot)
½ cup baby corns - cut into paper thin round slices
2-3 red radish - cut into slices or a tomato - cut into 8 pieces and pulp removed

1 capsicum - cut into ½" pieces
12-15 paper thin slices of unpeeled cucumber
4-5 lettuce leaves - torn into 1" pieces

MARINADE FOR THE VEGETABLES
½ cup white vinegar
½ cup ice cold water, lots of ice cubes
1 tsp salt, 1 tsp sugar

1. Mix all ingredients of the dressing till smooth. Keep in the refrigerator till serving time.
2. Mix vinegar with all the other ingredients of the marinade in a large bowl. Add carrots, baby corns, radish, capsicum, cucumber and lettuce. Keep in the fridge for 1-2 hours or till serving time.
3. At serving time, pick up the vegetables from the water and put on a clean kitchen towel. Pat dry and keep in the serving bowl. Arrange 1-2 lettuce leaves on the sides.
4. Add pineapple pieces and olives or cherries. Mix.
5. Pour the mustard dressing over it and gently mix. The dressing should not be mixed too well. Serve immediately.

Spicy Potato Salad with Sesame Seeds

A salad which goes well with an Indian meal.

Serves 4

½ kg (4 medium) potatoes
2-3 tbsp chopped mint (poodina) leaves
2-3 green chillies - deseeded & slit lengthways
½ cup fresh red anaar (pomegranate) ke dane
4 tbsp khatti mithi imli or amchur ki chutney, salt & pepper to taste
2 tsp til (sesame seeds) - lightly roasted on a tawa

1. In a large saucepan, heat water. Add washed potatoes. Cover & boil for 15-20 minutes till just soft. Keep checking inbetween with a knife to see if they have turned soft. Do not pressure cook or over boil them. Peel & slice them into ¼" thick rounds. Place in a big serving bowl & sprinkle salt and pepper while still warm. Toss gently.
2. Add anaar, mint leaves & green chillies.
3. Sprinkle chutney. Add half of the til seeds and toss lightly. Chill.
4. Transfer to a serving bowl and sprinkle the left over til seeds.

Thai Papaya Salad

Picture on inside front cover

Serves 4-6

3 cups grated hard, raw papaya (kachha papita)
1 tomato - cut into 8 pieces and deseeded
½ cup tender green beans (french beans or lobia or chawli) - sliced finely
¼ cup roasted peanuts - crushed coarsely

TAMARIND CHILLI DRESSING

1 tbsp tamarind pulp
1 tbsp soya sauce, 2 tbsp lemon juice
2 tbsp sugar, ½ tsp chilli powder, ½ tsp salt, or to taste
2 tbsp chopped coriander
3-4 green chillies and 1 flake garlic - pounded together

1. Mix all ingredients of the dressing together.
2. Put papaya and all other ingredients in a bowl. Add the dressing and mix well. Cover with a cling film and chill for at least one hour, so that the flavours penetrate. Serve topped with some roasted peanuts.

Tricolour Cream Cheese Salad

Serves 4-5

1 cup rajmah (red kidney beans) - boiled
1 cup macaroni - boiled
2-3 cups cucumber - cubed into small pieces
1 cup spring onions - chopped
½ cup capsicum - chopped

DRESSING
1½ cups curds (made from full cream milk and hung for 1-2 hours)
100 gms fresh cream
1 tsp mustard powder
salt & lemon juice to taste
milk as much as required
red & green food colours

1. Hand the curds in a muslin cloth for atleast 1 hour.
2. Beat the hung curds well with an electric egg beater or a wooden spoon so that it becomes smooth & no lumps remain.
3. Add salt, mustard powder & lemon juice. Mix well. Add cream. Mix lightly. If the dressing seems too thick, add some milk.
4. Divide into 3 parts.
5. To one part add boiled macaroni.
6. To the second part add rajmah & a drop of red colour. Mix well.
7. To the third part add capsicum, cucumbers, spring onions & a drop of green colour. Mix well.
8. To serve, arrange macaroni in the centre of the serving plate. Surround it with rajmah and lastly arrange the green layer surrounding the red layer of rajmah.

Note: The salad being tricolour looks good without any extra garnishing.

Cucumber Mousse

The salad has a rich cool texture and is always a great hit.

Serves 8-10

6 medium (6 cups grated) cucumber
1½ tbsp salt
4 tbsp vinegar
2½ cups curds prepared from ½ kg full cream milk
1 lemon jelly packet
2 cups chopped spring onion
1 tsp salt
1½ tsp pepper
2 tbsp chopped coriander leaves

GARNISHING
3-4 lettuce leaves - finely chopped

1. Hang curds in a muslin cloth for 1-2 hours.
2. Grate cucumbers. Mix with 1½ tbsp salt and 4 tbsp vinegar. Put into a colander, put a heavy plate (chakla) on top & leave for atleast 1 hour, so as to remove excess water from cucumbers.
3. Remove the plate & squeeze the cucumbers through a clean muslin cloth to get the last of the liquid away.
4. Dissolve jelly in 1¾ cups of hot water. Cool.
5. Mix hung curds with jelly and beat well.
6. Add spring onions, cucumbers, salt, pepper and coriander leaves.
7. Transfer to a wet jelly mould & set in the fridge for 5-6 hours.
8. Unmould, surround with finely chopped lettuce leaves & serve chilled.

Note: It is better to make the salad one day in advance so that it sets well.

Yoghurt Salad

An extremely delightful salad. Must give it a try!

Serves 8

1 cup finely chopped cabbage
½ cup chopped carrots (¼" cubes)
1 small boiled potato - chopped into ¼" cubes
¼ cup chopped cucumber (¼" cubes)
¼ cup shelled peas
½ apple - cut into small cubes without peeling
1 tbsp finely chopped mint leaves

YOGHURT DRESSING

2½ cups curd prepared from ½ kg full cream milk
1 tsp mustard powder - optional
1 tbsp powdered sugar, 1 tsp refined oil, salt, pepper to taste
150 gms fresh cream

GARNISHING

tomato rose - page 67

1. To prepare the dressing, hang curd in a thin muslin cloth for 1-2 hours.
2. Beat the curd well till smooth.
3. Add sugar, oil and mustard powder.
4. Gently mix in the cream. Keep dressing aside.
5. Boil 4 cups of water with 1 tsp salt and ½ tsp sugar.
6. Add carrots & peas. When peas are tender, add chopped cabbage. Remove from fire after ½ minute.
7. Strain. Keep the boiled vegetables in the strainer for 15-20 minutes to drain away all the water.
8. Add boiled vegetables, apple pieces, cucumber and mint leaves to the yoghurt dressing. Mix gently.
9. Add salt, pepper to taste. Add more sugar if desired.
10. Make a tomato rose a given on page 67 & arrange on a side of the salad. Arrange 2-3 mint leaves (dipped in ice cold water for 10 minutes) on the sides of the rose.

Cole Slaw (with egg)

A salad generally served with burgers, sandwiches and cutlets.

Serves 8

¾ cup mayonnaise sauce- recipe on page 74
50 gm (½ cup) cream, 1 flake garlic crushed - optional
½ of a medium cabbage - shredded into fine strips
1 thick carrot - grated into long pieces
1 tsp lime juice - to taste, salt & pepper to taste

1. Prepare mayonnaise as given on page 74.
2. Gently mix in the cream & crushed garlic. Keep aside.
3. Wash cabbage well. Cut into half & remove the hard core. Shred the cabbage finely into thin strips.
4. Peel & grate carrot, discarding the hard core.
5. Place the vegetables in a large bowl. Add mayonnaise. Toss with 2 forks until all the shreds are coated with the dressing. Chill.
6. At serving time, add lime juice, salt & pepper to taste. If salt is added earlier, the cabbage leaves water and the coleslaw becomes runny.

Cole Slaw (Eggless)

Serves 8

1 cup (200 gms) fresh cream - chilled
2 tbsp oil
1 tsp mustard powder
3 tsp lemon juice, 3 tsp powdered sugar
½ tsp salt, ¼ tsp pepper
1 flake garlic crushed - optional
½ of a medium cabbage - shredded
1 carrot - grated

1. Beat the chilled cream with all ingredients except cabbage & carrot, till it starts turning slightly thick and attains a **thick pouring** consistency. Do not beat any more.
2. Wash cabbage. Cut into half & remove the hard core. Shred cabbage finely into thin strips. Peel & grate carrot, discarding the hard core.
3. Place vegetables in a large bowl. Add cream. Toss with 2 forks until all the shreds are coated with dressing. Add more salt & pepper if desired. Chill.

Minty Spinach & Nut Salad

Serves 4-5

2 cups shredded spinach leaves (use only leaves & discard the stem)
1 cup shredded cabbage
½ cup thinly sliced capsicum
1 cup grated carrots
18-20 fresh mint (pudina) leaves - chopped
½ cup roasted peanuts

DRESSING
2 tbsp mayonnaise - page 70, 74
1 tsp vinegar
½ tsp salt
a dash of nutmeg powder (jaiphal)

1. Prepare mayonnaise dressing as given on page 70 or 74. Chill mayonnaise. Add all the other ingredients of the dressing & keep in the fridge.
2. Wash spinach & cabbage leaves. Keep on a clean kitchen towel to absorb water. Shred into thin long strips.
3. In a big utensil (paraat), mix both the shredded leaves, carrots, capsicum peanuts & chopped mint leaves.
4. Pour dressing over the vegetables & mix gently with 2 forks held in both the hands to avoid the vegetables getting mushy.
5. Chill for 1-2 hours before serving.

Note: It is a colourful salad requiring no garnishing.

Quick Tossed Salad

Tastes delicious with any ordinary meal.

Serves 6

½ cup chopped cabbage, ½ cup grated carrot
¼ cup chopped onion, ½ cup chopped tomatoes
½ cup halved grapes
½ cup orange segments

FRENCH DRESSING
2 tbsp oil
2 tbsp vinegar
salt & pepper - ½ tsp each
1 tsp sugar

1. Mix all fruits and vegetables.
2. Mix all ingredients of the French dressing & whisk well. Pour the dressing over the fruit and vegetable mixture.
3. Toss lightly. Add more salt and sugar if required. Chill.

Egyptian Delight

Serves 4-5

2 cups thinly shredded cabbage
1½ cups sprouted moong
1 cup chopped cucumber
1 cup peeled orange segments
1 recipe green cottage cheese dressing (1 cup) page 78

GARNISHING

some chopped coriander leaves, rings of cucumber and tomatoes

1. Mix cabbage, moong, cucumber & orange segments in a large bowl.
2. Pour the dressing over it gradually, mixing it lightly. Add just enough dressing to coat. Chill for 1-2 hours before serving.
3. Garnish with rings of tomatoes, cucumber chopped coriander leaves.

Note: The salad dressing is quite thick, but the cabbage leaves a little water on keeping. Hence make the salad 1-2 hours in advance. At the time of serving, mix well & decorate. Serve chilled.

Beetroot & Baby Onion Salad

Picture on Page 35

Serves 4

2 small beetroots
10 small baby onions - cut into paper thin slices
a few coriander or parsley leaves (dipped in ice cold water)- to garnish

DRESSING
1½ tbsp honey, 3 tbsp vinegar
1 tbsp oil, 2-3 flakes garlic - crushed, ½ tsp salt, ¼ tsp pepper

1. Pressure cook beets with 2-3 cups water to give 3 whistles. Cool. Peel & cut into thin slices. Cut each slice diagonally to get 4 triangles.
2. Cut onions into very thin slices with a sharp knife & put in ice cold water for 20 minutes. Separate the rings.
3. Mix all ingredients of the dressing in a small bowl. Put the beet pieces in large bowl and pour the dressing over it. Mix well. Keep aside.
4. At serving time, add the onion rings and mix lightly. Transfer to a serving dish. Sprinkle with parsley or coriander leaves.

Italian Corn & Pasta (Macaroni) Salad

Serves 4-5

1 cup boiled cooled macaroni or any other pasta
1 cup boiled cooled corn
½ cup chopped cucumber
½ cup chopped capsicum
½ cup sliced grapes or melon or orange segments
1 recipe Italian dressing (½ cup) page 77

1. Mix boiled macaroni, corn, cucumber, capsicum & fruit together in a bowl.
2. Pour the dressing and mix thoroughly. Chill.
3. Transfer to a serving dish. Garnish with some sliced cucumbers & fruit.

Note: A touch of fruit should always be given to this salad.

Chinese Sprouted Bean Salad with Pineapple

Serves 3-4

1½ cups sprouted beans (moong can be used or any other beans)
¼ cup cabbage - shredded
½ cup pineapple (tinned) - shredded
¼ cup grated carrot

DRESSING
1 tsp soya sauce
1 tbsp vinegar
1 tsp sugar
1 tbsp oil
1 tsp sherry (optional)
salt to taste, a pinch of ajinomoto

GARNISHING
tomato wedges & some chopped coriander leaves

1. In a bowl mix all the ingredients of the dressing together. Keep in the fridge.
2. Heat 2 cups of water with ½ tsp of salt. When the water boils, add the bean sprouts & cook uncovered for 1 minute. Drain well & cool. Put on a clean kitchen towel to absorb excess water.
3. Mix bean sprouts, cabbage, carrot & pineapple in a bowl and chill.
4. Just before serving, pour the dressing over the chilled vegetables. Toss lightly to mix.
5. Garnish with tomato wedges and chopped coriander leaves. Serve chilled.

Balkan Cucumber Salad

Serves 4-5

½ cup sprouted moong
2 cups cucumber peeled & cubed
1 cup thinly sliced onion
3/4 cup curds (from full cream milk)
½ cup (100 gm) fresh cream
1 cup chopped toasted walnuts
2 tsp honey or sugar
¼ cup finely chopped coriander leaves
salt & black pepper to taste

MINCE TOGETHER
½ cup spring onions
4-5 fresh mint leaves (pudina)
2 small flakes garlic (optional)

GARNISHING
2 hard boiled eggs
1 tomato - sliced into thin wedges
1 carrot - cut into match sticks
some lettuce leaves

1. Mince spring onions, garlic & mint leaves with 2 tsp curd in a mixer/spice grinder.
2. Peel and cube the cucumber & slice onions.
3. In a bowl mix curds, cream, minced mixture, coriander, honey, salt & pepper.
4. Add cucumber, sprouts & onions. Do not add walnuts.
5. Chill thoroughly. Mix walnuts just before serving.
6. Serve on a bed of lettuce leaves garnished with slices of tomatoes, boiled eggs & carrots.

Russian Salad

Picture on page 53

Serves 4

Mayonnaise (¾ cup) - page 74, 70
50 gm (½ cup cream)
12-15/1 cup french beans - threaded & cut into ¼" diagonal pieces
3 medium (1 cup) carrot - cut into ¼" pieces
1 big potato (½ cup) boiled potato - cut into ¼" pieces
½ cup peas - boiled
1 cup tinned pineapple or apple - chopped into small pieces

or

1 cup grapes - halved

GARNISHING
1 orange - unpeeled & cut into round slices
2-3 lettuce leaves

1. Boil 4-5 cups of water with 1 tsp salt and 1 tsp sugar. Add french beans, carrots and peas in boiling water and cook for 3-4 minutes till the peas are just done. Do not over boil.
2. When done, drain immediately and refresh by putting in ice cold water (so as to retain their colour). Strain. Keep in the strainer for 10 minutes.
3. Mix boiled vegetables, boiled potato and fruit in a large bowl.
4. Mix mayonnaie with cream. Pour the mayonnaise dressing gradually over the fruit and vegetable mixture, mixing lightly. Add just enough dressing to coat the vegetables.
5. Serve chilled decorated with a lettuce leaf. Arrange 3-4 unpeeled orange slices, slightly overlapping each other.

Lebanese Tabbouli or Tabbouleh

It is made from cracked wheat. Besides being highly nutritious, it is quick to prepare & very unusual in its taste.

Serves 3-4

1 cup dalia (cracked wheat)
1 cup paneer (cottage cheese)
2 medium tomatoes - deseeded & chopped finely
1 medium capsicum - chopped finely
1 medium onion - chopped finely
2-3 green chillies - chopped finely
1 tsp salt
3 tsp lemon juice
2-3 tsp minced mint leaves (pudina)
1-2 tbsp chopped coriander (dhania) leaves

GARNISHING
1 tomato - cut into wedges
1 capsicum - cut into rings
a few lettuce leaves

1. Soak dalia in water for 1 hour.
2. Strain & squeeze out the excess water from the dalia.
3. Chop tomatoes, capsicum, onion, green chillies very finely. Mix with the dalia.
4. Crumble paneer and add.
5. Add salt, pudina, dhania and lemon juice. Mix well.
6. Put it in a bowl. Press well and cover with a plate.
7. Chill for 2-3 hours.
8. To serve, unmould on to a platter decorated with lettuce leaves. Garnish with tomato wedges & capsicum rings.

Dips, Party Starters

&

Unusual Soup Accompaniments

Cheese Dip

Picture on page 36

Dips can be served with rolls, potato wafers, carrot or kheera sticks or any other starter.

Makes 1 small bowl

1 cup hung curds (2½ cups of curds from full cream milk hung in a muslin cloth for 2-3 hours)
2 tbsp cheese spread
100 gms fresh cream
1 medium onion - chopped very fine
1 medium capsicum - deseeded & chopped very fine
juice of 1 lemon
salt to taste and white pepper to taste

1. Beat the curd and cheese spread with an electric beater till smooth.
2. Mix cream gently.
3. Add all other ingredients & mix lightly. Chill.
4. Serve in a small bowl with starters.

Poodina Dip

1 cup hung curds (2½ cups of curds from full cream milk hung in a muslin cloth
for 2-3 hours)
100 gms fresh cream
2 tbsp ground pudina leaves & a few drops of green colour
juice of 1 lemon, salt to taste

1. Beat the curd with an electric beater till smooth. Mix cream gently.
2. Add all other ingredients and mix lightly. Chill. Serve in a small bowl.

Garlic Dip

1 cup hung curds (2½ cups of curds from full cream milk hung in a muslin cloth
for 2-3 hours)
100 gms fresh cream
2 tsp ground garlic, 1 tsp red chilli powder
juice of 1 lemon, salt to taste

1. Beat the curd with an electric beater till smooth. Mix cream gently.
2. Add all other ingredients & mix lightly. Chill. Serve in a small bowl.

Crunchy Rolls

Picture on page 36

12 pieces

1 cup dalia (cracked wheat)
150 gm paneer (cottage cheese) - mashed roughly (1 cup)
1 tsp salt, ½ tsp red chilli powder
2-3 green chillies - chopped fine
½ " piece ginger - chopped fine
1 tsp dhania (coriander) powder
½ tsp garam masala, 1 tsp amchur (dry mango powder)
2-3 tbsp chopped coriander leaves
1 tsp lemon juice
oil for frying

1. Soak dalia in water for 1 hour. Strain. Squeeze out excess water by pressing well.
2. Mix crumbled paneer and all other ingredients to the dalia. Mix well.
3. Form into balls or 1" long rolls. Flatten sides & deep fry 1 or 2 pieces at a time in hot oil till golden brown. Serve hot with soups.

Thord Man Khaophed (Thai)

Peanut -Corn Cutlets

12-14 *cutlets*

¾ cup raw corn (fresh or frozen)
¾ cup peanuts - roasted
½ cup potatoes - boiled & mashed
1 tsp red chilli powder
2 tsp soya sauce
1 tbsp chopped coriander leaves
4 tbsp cornflour
salt to taste
½ tsp baking powder
juice of 1 lemon

1. Put all the ingredients in the mixer except potatoes, cornflour & baking powder. Grind to a fine paste.
2. Mix potatoes, cornflour and baking powder to the above paste.
3. Shape into cutlets and deep fry.

Nacho Chips with Cheese Dip

Makes 40-45 chips

1½ cup maize flour (makki ka atta)
1 cup flour (maida)
2 tbsp oil
1 tsp salt
½ tsp ajwain

1. Mix both the flours, oil, ajwain & salt.
2. Knead into a dough with water.
3. Make small marble sized balls. Roll out into thin chappatis.
4. Prick the chappati well with a fork.
5. Cut into 4 pieces so as to get 4 triangular chips.
6. Deep fry on medium flame till they turn golden brown in colour.
7. To serve, place cheese dip in a bowl in the centre of a large plate surrounded by nacho chips.

Note: These chips can be made 5-6 days in advance & stored in an air tight container.

Garlic Toast

Serves 4-5

3 slices of bread
4-5 tsp salted butter (Amul)
1 tsp minced garlic paste
¼ tsp black pepper, ¼ tsp salt

1. Mix butter, salt, pepper & garlic paste.
2. Apply thinly on the bread slices.
3. Re-assemble the bread slices like the bread & wrap in an aluminium foil.
4. Bake in a hot oven at 200°C for 15-20 minutes.
5. Cut into 4-5 sticks. Serve hot with soups or as a snack.

Note: The bread slices can be sliced into 4-5 pieces & then baked.

Sesame Potato Triangles

Picture on page 71

Serves 6-8

5 slices of bread
1 cup boiled mashed potatoes
½ cup flour (maida)
1½ cubes or 40 gm (1/3 cup) grated cheese
a big pinch of baking powder
salt & pepper to taste
oil for frying, 1 tbsp til (sesame seeds)

1. Mix potatoes, flour, grated cheese, baking powder, salt & pepper. Put a little extra salt in the paste as it has to be spread on bread.
2. Cut each bread slice into 4 triangles. Cover each piece with the above mixture. Sprinkle til seeds generously.
3. Press lightly with the fingers.
4. Heat oil and fry till potatoes turn **brown** and the til seeds show nicely. Remove from oil on absorbent paper. Serve hot with any soup.

VAR/30358/12/01

NITA MEHTA'S BEST SELLING TITLES BY SNAB

COOKERY BOOKS

1. All-time favourite SNACKS* **
2. Best of CHINESE Vegetarian Cuisine* **
3. Breakfast & Brunch (Non Veg)
4. Breakfast Special
5. Cakes & Chocolates*
6. CHINESE Cooking for the Indian Kitchen
7. CHINESE Non Veg
8. Chutneys Squashes Pickles
9. Corn and Pasta
10. Dal & Roti* ***
11. Delicious Parlour ICE CREAMS
12. Desserts & Puddings* **
13. Different Ways with CHAAWAL**
14. Favourite Non Vegetarian Dishes
15. Flavours of INDIAN COOKING
16. Green Vegetables
17. Handi Tawa Kadhai
18. Healthy & Delicious FOOD FOR CHILDREN
19. Indian Vegetarian Cookbook (Paperback)
20. JHATPAT KHAANA-Vegetarian
21. Low Calorie Desserts
22. LOW CALORIE RECIPES Non Veg
23. Low Calorie Recipes**
24. MICROWAVE Non Veg Cookery
25. MICROWAVE Vegetarian Cookery* **
26. More PANEER
27. MUGHLAI Vegetarian Khaana*
28. NAVRATRI Special Recipes
29. PANEER All the Way* ** ***
30. Perfect Vegetarian Cookery (P.B)
31. SANDWICHES
32. SNACKS Non-Veg
33. Soups Salads & Starters
34. South Indian Favourites
35. Starters & Mocktails
36. Taste of KASHMIR
37. Taste of PUNJAB - Vegetarian
38. Taste of RAJASTHAN- Veg
39. The Art of BAKING
40. The Best of CHICKEN Recipes*
41. The Best of Vegetarian Dishes
42. Vegetarian Wonders (Paperback)

*Also available in Hindi, ** Also available in Gujarati, *** Also available in Bengali

For Details about *Nita Mehta* Cookery Books & Classes, Call: 6214011, 6238727 (DELHI)